He
Lives

Mary Ashton

Copyright © held by author 2019

About the Author: Mary Ashton

I was born in Yorkshire England and my father was a miner. My mother worked in the fields whenever there was planting or harvesting to be done.

In 1962, my husband's work took me to North Africa and since then I have spent most of my life in and out of different parts of Africa: lastly in and around Johannesburg, where I became a Born Again Christian and joined the Apostolic Church in 1982. I now attend International City Church on Netherhall Road Doncaster.

My poems relate to special experiences in my Christian walk, all have exciting stories of how God intervened in my life. One day I could write a book!

I pray you will be blessed and enjoy your walk with us through these pages.

Mary Ashton.

A State of Heart

The Lord doesn't want a stubborn heart
Or a heart that's filled with pride
The Lord doesn't want a selfish heart
It was for these that he died
He can't wait until you're perfect
In everything you do
The Lord just wants you as you are
The Lord is calling you.

The Lord seeks to find a humble heart
A broken heart that's willing
A heart that feels its shame and sin
And with new life needs filling
A heart that aches for another chance
To start life once again
The Lord says: "Come, give me your grief
Let me take your pain".

The Lord knows you'll never make it
He sees you struggle on your own
That's why he calls to tell you
You need never be alone
Jesus truly loves you
He died to give you life
He wants to be your husband
To take you as his wife.
Jesus loves you, truly loves you
That's why he died on Calvary
Your sin-filled heart was condemned to hell
But his love cried: "God take me!"

His blood was shed to save you
He died to set you free
He took your selfish, sin-filled heart
And gave it life anew
He wants your hopeful, thankful heart
The Lord is calling you.

<u>SURRENDER</u>

There's a feeling of nearness
When I can see no one is there
There's a warmth of love around me
That makes me kneel in prayer
How can you want me, Jesus,
Why choose this life of mine
My life is worthless rubbish
There are better lives than mine.

Still I feel you, close beside me
Your light is all around
My heart can hear your loving words
My ear yet hears no sound
How can you love me, Jesus,
My heart is made of stone
I've learned to trust nobody
I'll manage on my own.

And yet you stay beside me
I'm tempted to give in
Your loving hand to guide me

Your blood frees me from sin
I want to trust you, Jesus,
Though my hope is very thin
As I open up my heart's gate
I feel all your love flow in.

Oh! My blessed, glorious Saviour
It's wonderful to know
You can take a woman just like me
And teach her love can grow
From a little tiny feeling
Came this wonderful sensation
From an absolutely nothing
Came this marvellous elation
Teach me to be worthy
My constant prayer will be
Let me give God all the glory
Let his love shine through me.
                    Amen

GIFTS OF LOVE

Do we ever stop and wonder
At the fullness of God's love
Of the thoughtful things
He does for us each day
Do we ever stop to count
As each minute passes by
Of the love He shows
That words just couldn't say.

Oh! I want to tell him that I love him

I want to praise his holy name
I want to dance and clap
And let my praises ring
I want to sing and cry and worship
I want to give him all my love
And of my life, I'll say
You are the King.

In my life I want to thank Him
As He demonstrates his love
When he sends a cloud
To cool the hottest day
In my heart I'm deeply grateful
When his spirit, like a dove,
Takes my hand and guides me,
Lest I stray.
Oh! I want to praise and thank him
I want to tell him that I care
I want to tell the world
That Jesus is my King
I want to tell him that I love him
That I know he's always there
And of my life,
I'll give him everything.

It's just great to bless and praise him
To appreciate his love
When I start, I never want to stop
How I have to just admire
How he knows me heart's desire
And he makes me gifts
With cherries on the top.

My lips are full of praising
My hands are always rising
My heart's so full
Its bursting at the seams
I want to tell him that I love him
I want to give him all my love
And of my life,
I've everlasting dreams.

TO JACQUALINE

My dearest little daughter
How can I let you know
Although I love you very much
God loves you more, and so
He sent his Son to die for you
A price so hard to pay
So listen love, don't turn your back
Just close your eyes and say
"Thank you, God, for saving me"
It's not so hard to pray.

My dearest sweetheart, little girl
I've cried so much for you
You can play, and ride, and roller-skate
But, love, please know God too
Learn to talk to Jesus
He is God's loving Son

He loves all little children
He won't stop you having fun

With Jesus riding at your side
You'll "clear round" all the jumps
And even if you do fall off
You won't feel any bumps
You'll never get downhearted
You're never even bored
Life is so full of living
With Jesus as your Lord.

Please, sweetheart, just try it
Just close your eyes and see
Know you're doing it for you!
Don't do it just for me
Please, Lord, melt her little heart
Tell her what to do
Please, Lord, help her make a start
Keep her safe in You.

SAILING

Can you imagine a little boy
With a plastic sail boat for a toy
Up and down
Side to side
It's sails his imaginations tide
It's a pirate ship in his little mind
He can hear the cannonballs rattle

It's a big destroyer making a wake
As it charges on into battle
It's a yacht in a basin, peaceful, at rest
It's a racing boat, speeding fast, only the best
Many hours he can play with his plastic boat
But plastic soon cracks then it won't stay afloat.
Can you imagine that little boy
His boat now I real, no longer a toy
Up and down
Side to side
His poor stomach heaves
As big rollers they ride
He's a smart sailor now, fighting wars for his nation

Steel under his feet as he stands at his station
His eyes bright, alert
He's still eager for battle
He's determined to win, as the first bullets rattle
His body taut, ready
His heart young and brave
He's so proud he's a man now
He's had his first shave.

Can you imagine our young man now
On a ship as big as a city
Up and down
Side to side
Let us pray, let us ask God to be by his side
As these men run about on this ship made of steel
On this ship so big, so fantastic
It takes one bomb dropped in the right place
Then it sinks!

Like a boat made of plastic.
Once again imagine our little boy
His face is radiant, full of joy
Up and down
Side to side

He sways' with the chorus
His arms open wide
His life here is ended
It had hardly begun
Someone is crying
He was some Mother's Son
But there's one Son in heaven
He came down to save
In this case he came for the young and the brave
Jesus is there, he gave his life too
He died for our sin, for me and for you
He has shown us that death's not the end of the story
For those who believe, there's eternal glory.

<u>RESTING</u>

I stood by his throne of mercy
I stood by his throne of grace
Such stillness, such peace, such beauty, such love
I'm longing to gaze at his face.

I bow by his seat of judgement
I bow by his seat of power

Such goodness, such kindness, forgiveness and love
I wait on him hour by hour.

I kneel by his knee of compassion
I kneel by his knee of care
Such gentleness, patience
Understanding and love
I'm so thankful that I can be there.

I sit at the feet of my Saviour
I sit at the feet of my King
All my praise, all my worship, all my life and my love
To Jesus I give everything.
I rest in the presence of Jesus
I rest in the presence of Him
Secure in his faithfulness
Secure in his love
His love-light will never grow dim.

Join me by his throne of mercy
Join me by his seat of grace
Such stillness, such peace, such beauty, such love
Join me as I gaze on his face.

GUESS WHO

My love has a heart
As big as a mountain
My love is so gentle
So tender, so kind
My love has a way of always just knowing
What's in my heart, what's on my mind.

My love has a voice loving and tender
The sound brings me comfort when I'm in despair
My love gives me peace
He knows just how to tell me
Wherever I'm going, he'll always be there.

My love has a body, to always protect me
With his hands he constantly shows me his love
When he stands beside me
There's a tingle inside me
My love is the kind of love dreams are made of.

Jesus has a heart as big as a mountain
Jesus has a voice that is loving and kind
Jesus gave of his body to always protect me
Jesus' love is the purest love I will ever find.
Jesus' love is so real I can almost touch it
Jesus' love makes me tremble, the power is so strong
When he stands beside me
As the joy mounts inside me
I whisper "I love you" and sing a love song.

Jesus' love is so great there is plenty left over
God so loved the world
That he gave us his Son
When we sinned he cried for us
In our worst he died for us
Jesus' love is the greatest love
Sent from above.

I love him, I love him, I love him, I love him
How else can I tell him, what more can I say?
I will walk in his footsteps
I will be his disciple
I will run the great race
I will try for the prize
There's only one way I can be a disciple
There will be Jesus love for you
Lighting my eyes.

CANT STOP SINGING

I want to sing about Jesus
I want to feed on his name
I want to sing about Jesus the King
Christ Jesus, God's Son
Praise His name.

There are so many songs about Jesus
It's a wonder they don't sound the same
If sung from the heart
He won't mind at all
He just wants our love
Praise His name.

Oh! Wonderful, wonderful Jesus
I'm so grateful, so thankful you came
As God's Son you came
Without blemish or spot
And died for our sins
Praise His name.
You freed me from sin loving Jesus
You paid a price I couldn't pay
You hung on the cross
And then conquered death
To sit at God's side
Praise His name.

I could sing all night about Jesus
I imagine his suffering, his pain
It's hard to believe you did all that for me
I'm so thankful, I sing
Praise His name.

Let me give you my life, precious Jesus
Let me tell everyone that you came
Let them know they've been saved
By the price of his blood
With hands lifted, sing
Praise His name.

Now I have a new life in Jesus
I feed on the bread of his name
I give thanks to God
For sending his Son
Christ Jesus, the King
Praise his name.

TRUTH IS

Is this really real?
Are all these strange happenings happening to me?
Is this how I should feel?
Am I ready?
Is this how God wants me to be?
If I hadn't known
If I hadn't been shown
By now I would have presumed it was all imaginary.

But God touched me, I know!
It wasn't the kind of feeling I could invent
It was a kind of glow
A magnetized feeling
I'm sure it could only have been heaven sent
I wanted to pray
I wanted to say so many words but couldn't
My body felt already spent.

Sometimes, I think, if I pinch myself
Surely I would just come awake
Sometimes, I think, I must be asleep
And all I need is a really good shake
But then I see you, then I see you
So many people dreaming my dream
That's too hard to take.

I feel in a trance
The kind of sensation that makes me feel
I'm walking on air
It's a slow motion dance

My partner? A presence I feel when nobody's there
I say, I love you, he loves me too
Then we move in a rapture
A mutual loving without any care.

Thank God! It's real
This beautiful happiness, tranquil peacefulness
Really is me
Praise God it's real
This waiting knowingness, glorious glowingness
Really is me
I want to sing, praise to Jesus my King
Giving my life, giving my love
Giving all, as he wants it to be.

EYES OF A CHILD

God is such a wonder
I think he's really funny
In the summer he makes flowers bloom, then
The bees can get the honey
When it comes to winter
And you're nose you've got to wipe
Wouldn't you know, it's just the time
He makes all the lemons ripe.
The honey and the lemons in recipes of old
Are just the right ingredients for fighting off a cold.

When it's hot in summer
He sends a cooling breeze

And just as if by accident
The leaves are on the trees
He just smiles because he knows
An accident it's not!
He put them there so we could find
A lovely shady spot.
He gives us sheep that grow the wool
To keep us nice and warm
He lets us watch the clouds build up
To warn us of a storm
When we think the rain will never stop
He shows us that's not so
By painting on the rainclouds
A lovely bright rainbow.

Every day's like Christmas
We get gifts galore
You only have to look around
You're in His present store
I really think he's wonderful
I really think he's funny
All he wants is love from us
We can't pay him with money.

The best is yet to come, you know
God created you and me
He made us in his likeness
He gave us eyes to see
Why I think he's funny
Why I said so from the start
He also put this love for Him
Inside my little heart

Yes, I think he's wonderful
This great God up above
All he wants from us is that
We give him back his love.

WHY ME

How many times over the years
Have you listened to voices, choking back tears?
Full of wonder, truly amazed
Voices trembling, sounding dazed
Asking, "Why Me, Lord?"

I've looked back on my life
I'm shattered to find it was wasted
I'm glad it's all left behind
There's nothing I know of to give me a clue
Did I say something?
What did I do? "Why me, Lord?"

I was hungry to feed on something I'd heard
I was hungry to dine on the bread of his word
Not noticing friends lost on the way
The feeling was urgent
I wanted to say "Why me, Lord?"

I listened to all about goodness and grace
I listened with tears streaming, wetting my face
I heard, "One perfect man died on the cross
The Son of God"

My gain was his loss
My sin was so heavy He had to die
Now I'm forgiven – Why? Why? Why?
Why me Lord?

I beg you humbly
Let me give you the glory
Please let me tell everybody your story
Let me tell how the Lamb for sinners was slain
The Son of God, Christ Jesus, his name
I have to hurry, the bible says
We're already moving in these latter days
Let ME Lord.

I beg, I beseech you, let ME be your host
Fill ME with the power of your Holy Ghost
I'll put on the whole armour
I'll get on my way
I won't waste a second
I'll start this very day
I'll serve you until I'm at heaven's gate
When you as "Who?"
I'll be happy to state
Why! Me, Lord!

PRAYERS ANSWERED

Hallelujah, praise the Lord
I can trust in his word
As each prayer is answered
I can sing, praise the Lord.

Hallelujahs I sing
Praise to Jesus, my King
Why, oh why should he love me?
Praise the Lord, praise the Lord.

My prayers are being answered
Every request
Each one as the Lord decides
For Jesus knows best
We can't make things happen
Not woman nor man
Only God makes things happen
So let's wait for his plan.

So I sing Hallelujah
Praise the Lord, praise the Lord
I give thanks to my saviour
As I trust in his word.

MANY CHRISTMASES

No room, no room, no room at the inn
No room for Mary with Jesus within
Yes, I understand the time must be near
But I am so busy, you can't come in here.

No room, no room, no vacancies dear
My rooms are all full, I must make it clear
Yes your time is now, but I've told you before
I really am busy, I must close the door.

No room, no room, should they try once more
Mary was burdened with the baby she bore
No I haven't got time, I can't help you now
Go sleep in the stable with the donkey and cow.

Jesus is coming, said Mary, the pain on her brow
Jesus is coming, the time is right now!
The Son of God came in the stable that night
With the lowliest creatures to witness the sight
We're so full of life when we begin
Carrying the Bible with Jesus within
But we soon find out as we go door to door
They are so busy, they've said so before.

They've got room in their lives for every small chore
For knitting or sewing or painting the door
They've got room in their lives for all kinds of sin
But no room for Mary with Jesus within.

But we will find one who won't turn us away
They don't want to be troubled, but hear what we say
Because Jesus is ready, yes you have guessed
Jesus is born there, that house will be blessed.

HARVEST TIME

How hard is it for those first drops of rain to penetrate
the land
As the sun beats down, baking the soil hard, like an
iron band
That poor drop of rain soon disappears
No sign to say it was there
Sun and heat and heavy dust, permeate the air.

More drops of rain, now a steady flow
The land begins to yield
What was hard and barren wilderness
Becomes once again green field
Signs of new birth as flowers bloom
And corn begins to grow
Hearts look on to the harvest
Love and smiles will overflow.

One by one heavenly raindrops fall
Spiritual rain from above
In early times it was hard to bring hopes of joy and
peace and love
But in these last days
As the raindrops fall

We see rivers and rivers of waters
We see the effects on the hard baked world
We're amazed at our Sons and our Daughters.

It's harvest time, let us sing and rejoice
Let hope come alive once again
Give thanks to God
Rejoice in His word
Thank God for his spiritual rain
How great is the harvest, how bountiful
The children all faces upturned
To receive from the Son those comforting rays
Taking food for the life they've so yearned
With arms reaching out
Dressed in bright array
Washed clean with a sweet perfume
Give thanks to the Father
All glory to God
Jesus is coming soon.

THE POWER

I wonder at the power of God
How his word became creation
When He said, there was land and sea
Every ocean, every nation
By his power all the universe is held in space
Until God casts it down again
By the power of His will.

I wonder at the love of God
He is the only One
Who else would love the world so much
He could sacrifice His Son?
He looked down and saw his creation steeped in sin
Only the power of the love of God
Could restore it once again.

I wonder at the power of the love of God
He sent his Son to save
Only the power of His love in Jesus
Brought Lazarus from his grave
Peter walked on water, when he didn't think he ought
See what became of Jonah
When he, by that fish was caught.

I wonder at the power of the love of God
The mystery of His plan
To know of His creation shows me
Just how small I am
It's impossible to understand or know why He should
care
I only know that when I pray
He lets me know He's there.

That's when I know the power of God
And wonder can it be?
The power of the universe
Has got a use for me
I kneel and tremble, waiting, for the power of His word
Then He moves me by that power
When He knows His voice I've heard.

How great is the power of the love of God
We can't possibly understand
All things are his creation
All things He has planned
By His love He sent His Son,
from sin to set us free
The God of the impossible
Cares that much for you and me!

DEAR MUM

I'd like to say thanks
For the many ways you've shown your love to me
I'd like to say thanks
For the things you do that come so naturally
You're always there when I need a smile
To take the kids or chat a while
I have to admit, I like your style
Thanks Mum.

I'd like to say thanks
For the many years you've struggled for us alone
I'd like to say thanks
For the special way you made our house a home
The many times you'd sit and wait
Yell at us when we came in late
You showed us love, I think you're great
Thanks Mum.

Now I'd like to thank God
For making us a Mum like you

I'm sure he looked down, nodded His head and said
'That'll do'
I bet He smiled with the greatest pleasure
As He thought what to do with this great treasure
So full of God's love, too much to measure
Thanks Mum.

I've just got to say thanks
But I could go on all day
Just saying 'thanks' and thinking of special things to
say
Thanks for showing us what Mother's love can do
Thanks for letting God's love shine through you
Thanks for all our trials you pulled us through
I want you to know – we love you too
Thanks Mum.

A REAL JESUS FAN

I go to meet him on a Sunday
I talk about him all day Monday
Read about him on a Tuesday
Tuesday really is, my good news day
Wednesday everything is fine
Morning and evening He is mine
I could talk to Him all day
He has time to hear me say
"Please do this" or "Please do that"
It's always nice to have a chat
Thursday I wake up with the dawn
Screw up my eyes and stretch and yawn

Then I remember He is there
So I kneel and say a little prayer
Friday starts another weekend
So I talk it over with "My friend"
Off to the shops to fill my platter day
That's all I can think to do with Saturday
But joy oh joy it is the one day
I know tomorrow will be Sunday.

Life

Praise and thankfulness
Joy and rejoicing
Great feelings of gladness
Today I am voicing
This love overflowing from deep in my heart
Am I the only one?
Am I apart?
Does anyone else find this joy just in living?
Does anyone else find this joy just in giving?
Not giving out things, just love from inside
Giving out smiles which push frownings aside
Let everyone know I'm happy, I'm free
I love everybody because Jesus loves me.

ME, JUST THINKING

Just thinking
Of soldier ants marching
Of grains of sand on the shore
Of how many people praying tonight
Maybe a million or more
Can you imagine?
Just stop and think
How great that sound must be
A million people praising God
And one of them – is me.

I was just thinking
Well hoping maybe
If I could persuade you and you
And the rest of that million
Could turn to their friends
And each one added just two
Can you imagine?
Just stop and think
What a magnificent sound that would be
Three million people praising God.
And one of them – is me.

I was just thinking
If we worked hard each day
Sharing our love in this way
Three million people
Spreading the word
Each bringing one soul to pray
Can you imagine?

Just stop and think
How victorious that sound would be
Six million, twelve million
Soon the whole world
And one of them still – would be me.

I was just thinking
Getting carried away
My mind can't imagine the sight
The whole world praying and praising God
Everyone getting it right
Can you imagine?
Just stop and think
What salvation then we would see
With life eternal
Seeing His face
One of them – Would be me.

So, I was just thinking
Just thanking God
That somebody chose to tell me
I'll look for that someone to tell the good news
The total then will be three
Can you imagine?
Just stop and think
A share in God's love, great and true
A share in the sound
Of the world praising God
The other one there – could be you.

WONDERFUL SAVIOUR

This saviour of mine is wonderful
He looks down from heaven above
There's nothing impossible for Him to do
All His gifts are given with love
His love is impossible for me to hide
In all my needs, He does provide
When I needed life, that's when He died
Oh what a wonderful saviour.

This saviour of mine is Almighty God
He controls the heaven and earth
While doing all this He can still see me
Though unworthy, He gave me worth
His love is impossible for me to hide
In all my needs He does provide
He is my bridegroom, I am His bride
Oh what a wonderful saviour.

This saviour of mine is Lord of Lords
He sits at the Father's right hand
At His name the angels in heaven obey
They rush to do his command
His love is impossible for me to hide
In all my needs He does provide
When I call on His name, He's by my side
Oh what a wonderful saviour.

This saviour of mine needs something from me
He wants my voice and my will

He wants me to tell you He loves you too
For you He's waiting still
With His love inside you, there's nothing to hide
In all your needs He will provide
Once you've tasted His goodness, you'll know why I cried
Oh what a wonderful saviour.

BETTER LATE

It's never too late to know the Lord
It's never too late to hear His word
Our sins are forgiven, that's understood
The debt had been paid, by the price of His blood
He died on the cross our sins to relieve
Now all you have to do is believe
Read the Bible, hear in His word
It's never too late to know the Lord.

Do you feel lost but don't know why?
Do you feel so lonely sometimes you could cry?
Do you feel empty, frustrated, down?
Do you feel you'd just like to get out of town?
Don't be discouraged, don't be misled
There was hope for Lazarus and he was dead
Read the Bible, hear in His word
It's never too late to know the Lord.

He will be with you wherever you go
Just knock on the door and say hello
Tell Him your troubles
Tell Him your fears

31

Tell Him things you've had bottled inside you for years

As you tell Him your heartache, He will relieve
Then you'll find it easy just to believe
Read the Bible, hear in his word
It's never too late to know the Lord.

Once you have repented before the Lord
Open the Bible and hear His word
You'll find your life full
A glorious sensation
Everyone in church becomes a relation
You feel yourself cleansed
Your sins washed away
You'll see your old friends
And you'll hear yourself say
Read the Bible, hear in His word
It's never too late to know the Lord.

GOOD NEWS

He lives, He lives
I saw Him plain as plain can be
He lives, He lives
He's alive, He showed Himself to me
Yes, I know that He was crucified
Yes, I know they made sure that He died
Yes, I know you'll find out if I've lied
I know He lives.

He lives, He lives
Don't ask me how it came to be
He lives, He lives
It's as much a mystery to me
I was crying, burdened down with care
Then I looked up and He was there
His voice, I'd know it anywhere
I know He lives.

He lives, He lives
Questions, questions
I can't answer now
He lives, He lives
Who am I to know the why's or how
Yes, I was standing next to you
Some of his blood fell on me too
I died inside, oh yes I knew
And yet He lives.

He lives, He lives
My heart is full of humble adoration
He lives, He lives
I need no earthly explanation
When He spoke He told me
"Go tell the others, let them know"
For those who doubt the empty tomb will show
My Lord, my Master, Jesus, God!
My saviour lives.

DUET OF LOVES

Soul
Lord Jesus how I need you, Lord Jesus how I need you
As I stumble in the darkness, my sin stain I must hide
As I tremble cold and lonely with no-one to love me
only
I long to have a someone to stand here by my side.

Jesus
I will never leave You, I will not forsake you
With love I hold my hands to you, my arms are open
wide
I will never leave you, I will not forsake you
My love endures forever, I'm right here by your side.

Soul
Dear God I've lost my way now, Dear God if I could
pray now
Dear God I've gone so far away, I'd call you if I could
But I have been so bad now, the chances I have had
now
I'm beyond forgiveness my sin is red as blood.

Jesus
I will never leave you, I will not forsake you
As you hear Me calling, turn and come to Me
I will never leave you, I will not forsake you
Lift your eyes to heaven, My love light you will see.

Soul
Dear god it is wasted this life you've given me
In this world no love, no hope, only selfishness I see

I'm worthless, I give up now there's no more to be said
Wait! As I prepare to end it all I see light ahead.

Jesus

I will never leave you, I will not forsake you
You are My creation and I love you endlessly
I will never leave you, I will not forsake you
I hear you and will save you as your heart calls out to me

Soul

Lord Jesus, I can feel your love a new life beckons me
As I lift my hand to take Your hand, a miracle I see
Because You died You saved my life, my sin stain washed away
Use my life, let Your love light shine, let others find a way.

Jesus

I will never leave you, I will not forsake you
Listen as I call your name, My love is in My voice
I will never leave you, I will not forsake you
As each soul is saved in heaven the angels will rejoice.

Together

I will never leave you, I will not forsake you
I give you this promise, as with love our hearts entwine
I will never leave you, I will not forsake you
We'll walk life's road together, as you join your life in mine.

TEENAGERS

How young girls giggle and make lots of noise
But remember that virgins can also be boys
Some are foolish, some are wise
Means not only girls, it applies to the guys.

When young people start growing, they want to stay '
cool'
No more going to Church or Sunday school
With disco dancing and dating in fashion, why think of
Jesus?
He cools of the passion.

It's fun to party along with the crowd
It's not easy to think when the music is loud
The flash of the lights, the smoke and the beat
No thoughts of danger, no thoughts of sorrow
Why think of Jesus, we'll do that tomorrow.

But these young folk knew Jesus when they were small
And he has never left them at all
He sees their behaviour, He hears all their lies
His heart is so sad, that poor Jesus cries
He's beside them and sees how they struggle through
life
His heart aches to help in their trouble and strife.

As their standards become lower and life becomes hell
Against parents and teachers and laws they rebel
They get caught in the whirlpool of their own self
destruction

They can't listen as friends try to give them instruction
The drinking and smoking and drugs they seemed
"WOW!"
Has finally destroyed them, so who wants them now?

There's Jesus still waiting to save every sinner
Whoever calls on His name is surely a winner
Call out "Jesus please help me, please save me from
sin"
Open your heart, bid Jesus 'come in'
Pour out your problems, your heartache, your pain
Jesus gives a new life
Become born again.

But like the wise virgins, keep oil in your lamp
You can't light the light if your matches get damp
Read your Bible, read of His promise for you
God wrote the Bible and God's word is true
The first call to Jesus must be your own
But from then on know, you are never alone.
As you follow Jesus and keep to His rule
Your old friends may laugh and say you're a fool
They may tease you and taunt you
With words try to break you
Jesus has promised, He will never forsake you.

Now you've made your decision, let nothing spoil
Remember, fools were the ones out looking for oil
Keep your eyes on Jesus
Keep your gaze firm and steady
When Jesus says 'come'
You be the ones ready

Who knows the time, the hour, the day
We know Jesus said, "He is the way"

Supposing He comes in the middle of night
Supposing He comes and your lamps not alight
He lets the wise in, then looks round for some more
But He can't see your light, so He closes the door!
Be wise and be ready
Let this message show you
Don't come late crying "Lord"
He will say, "I don't know you"
You won't need to drop out with Jesus inside
Say you have Jesus, say it with pride
Jesus will fill you with gifts from above
Spiritual gifts of forgiveness and love
The one who ignores this must be a fool
It's with Jesus to heaven
If you want to be cool!

HIS CALLING

I thirst, I hunger
I'm pushing the pace
Sometimes I feel as if I'm in a race
I make up my mind
I'm going no more
Then the Spirit anoints me
As I kneel on the floor.

I cry, I'm so sad
Then I'm in rapture
I get messages coming up out of the scripture
Put on the whole armour, that bit is true
Where am I going? What must I do?

I feel lost, I'm bewildered
But as I'm feeling down
Pure joy bubbles up, replacing my frown
I get so confused, I don't know where I'm going
But I must go on, not question, no knowing.

WITH MY LOVE

When you are crying, I will comfort
When you're hurting, I will care
When you're busy, I will wait for you
When you need me, I'll be there
When you're lost, My love will guide you
When you need, I will provide for you
When you're lonely, I'm beside you
When you need me, I'll be there.

When you're joyful, dancing singing
Oh what a joy it gives to Me
When you're voice with praises singing
Enjoying freedom to be free
It fills My heart with purest love
I'll gladly take the pain

My love is such, I'll gladly die
To set you free again.

As I look on with patience
And wait, My love to give
As I set each day before you
And watch you as you live
With all this world has got to offer
It's wonderful to see
You enjoy the peace and love that flows
When you're talking just to Me.

That's when I want to touch you
When my love will overflow
When I fill you with my loving
Joy and peace and love will grow
When you're crying, I will comfort
When you're hurting, I will care
When you're busy, I will wait for you
When you need me, I'll be there.

JUST BECAUSE OF JESUS

Before You came, time was, I knew it not
Before You came, joy was, I knew it not
Before, You came, love was, I knew it not
Never, was my time, never again
To think of Joy would bring to my mind, only pain
And as for love, that word to me was just a name
Life to me, was empty days, before You came.

Time and joy and love are treasure rare
Time wasted, seeking earthly pleasures, finding care
Time and time again, would find me in the fowler's
snare
Surely life was meant for living more than this
I would wait, inviting death to bring his kiss
Oh life, why must I struggle on in vain
Life, you see, was empty days before You came.

Then You came, time flew by as if on wings
Then You came, bringing joy and my heart sings
Then you came, in love, such love that only Jesus
brings
What is time, to me a fleeting minute
A thought is everlasting joy with Jesus in it
And as for love, consuming love in Jesus' name
My life will never be the same
Because You came.

That day, when time is ended, over there
With joy I thank my Jesus for His answer to my prayer
This love we feel, in words we try to capture
Together we'll be caught in timeless rapture
With joy and love we'll sing and praise His holy name
We'll say
"Thank you Jesus, this is just because You came.

IMAGINATIONS FLIGHT

A family resting after a picnic
Mum and Dad looking on with pride
As the children play, there's one little lad
His arms pointing straight out from his side
He's running around, bobbing and weaving
Making a noise with his mouth
He's lost in space, transmitting! Receiving!
He's on missions, North and South.

He's an aircraft enjoying the freedom of space
As he speeds away, then back
He's an old fashioned 'Two Wing' looping the loop
He's an old 'Spitty' under attack
Who knows how many 'Dog fights' are going on in his
mind's eye
Who knows the thoughts of this little lad?
As he enjoys the freedom of the sky.

The boy always wanted to be a pilot
So he read all the books he could get
He fancied himself at the controls
Flying low, in some Super jet
He studied hard, got his qualifications
His dreams were coming real
He joined the forces with its regulations
Still he did all his training with zeal.

At his passing out, his parents were there
As he marched, they looked on with pride
Tears pricked their eyes as they gazed at their son

This time arms stiff, down by his side
As time passed by, with hard work and training
Our boy turned into a man
So full of life, no one heard him complaining
He flies all the hours he can.

Suddenly the country was thrown into war
Forces briefed, ready to go
So he kissed his new wife, and his Mum and Dad
When he'd see them next
He didn't know
But they shared something special
This man and his loved ones, something not all pilots
had
They had Jesus to give them assurance
The best cover they ever had
They shared a prayer to God for safe keeping
They each voiced their faith in Him
There were tears but a feeling of quiet acceptance
Knowing soon, they'd be together again.

Our pilot met many men young and strong
Some ashamed to be trembling with fear
So he showed them how he'd got special protection
He was safe knowing Jesus was near
He told of how God sent His son to save men
He'd faced battles alone, against sin
How He took every sin and buried it with Him
Then He rose back to life once again.

As he told the story, hour by hour
The love in his eyes was aflame

He told of the healings, the strength and the power
There is just in using His name
So they believed in the wonder of Jesus
And salvation they have in God's love
It's a blessing to know, as these men are flying
If they go, they will stay up above.

FOR ILONA
Young soldiers in their training
Their lives have just begun
One of them is Andrew
Henry and Ilona's son
Our country needs defending
They have but one son to send
Help him to be brave Lord
Let him know You are his friend.

There are many people praying
For soldiers brave and true
Many parents with a need
To put their trust in You
Give these boys great courage Lord
Make them brave and strong
We all pray to You Lord
Their absence won't be long.

But each night, dear God, I know
Every mother's prayer will be
"Keep my baby safe and well,
And send him back to me.

THE LIFELINE

Dear God, what have I done?
Have I fallen out of grace?
Dear Lord, I want to see the light shine from Your face
Dearest Jesus, help me
I don't want to be alone
Lord, I feel so helpless
I'm falling like a stone.

Jesus, Jesus, help me!
Choose where I will land
Jesus, let me reach out
For the safety of Your hand
Jesus, I am begging on my hands and knees
Jesus as I call Your name
Won't you help me please?

Thank God, thank God for Jesus
Praise God he sent His Son
To have a friend like Jesus
He came to save us, everyone
 He lifts me up, He feeds me
His spirit takes my pain
Let me hang on to the lifeline
Of the power of Jesus' name.

PROBLEMS

Because it seems so difficult
To hear God's word today
Because it seems so difficult
To bow our heads and pray
Because it seems so difficult
To let one and one be two
Because it seems so difficult
Here's what we must do
Just trust in the lord
He will show us today
Just wait on the Lord
He's truth, the life, the way
Through the Holy Spirit
He will move us, one by one
We are just the instruments
By which God's work is done.

SPECIAL

So you think I'm special
Tell me, what can you see?
What is there that can be called
'Special' in me?
I didn't feel special, I had no special name
Only you called me special
The day that you came
God's love makes me special
Dear Lord, I can see
It's the flame of this Jesus love
Burning in me.

The day that God kindled
This love in my heart
That made me special, set me apart
Ok, so I'm special, supposing it's true
God's love makes me special
And His love for you
I like being special
Dear God let it be
Let the great love of Jesus
Shine specially through me.

WONDERMENT

It's strange to find how I look with new eyes
I'm acutely aware of the blue of God's skies
I'm aware of the detail of perfect creation
As I pause to study
I get a sensation of absolute wonderment.

How can I understand
With nothing but words, God created land
I just stand in amazement
I can't understand how, with so much to do
He can think of me now
I'm so unimportant, yet I'm part of His plan
Then I try to think out the creation of man.

But it's too much for me
So let me just stare
I thank God for His greatness
Then rest in His care.

TO THE HEALER

Dear Jesus, I want to say
I'm thankful that You came
I'm so grateful that You came to earth
To heal the sick and lame
You cast out devils
Raised the dead
You caused the blind to see
There's a little voice inside me, crying
Jesus, please heal me.

Dear Jesus, it says 'by faith' a person is made well
Is it in Your faith in us, or ours in You
I can never really tell
You changed my life
You saved my soul
Poured all Your love in me
There's this nagging voice insisting
Lord Jesus, please heal me.

Dear Jesus, it says that You stand knocking
I must open the door
If I ask Our Father in Your name
I get all I want and more
You came to earth
Was crucified
For sinners, just like me
How dare I have the cheek to ask
Lord Jesus, please help me.

Dear Jesus, let me change my tune

Forgive me once again
Compared with suffering I caused You
What's my one little pain?
I love you, let me serve You
I give my life to Thee
Forget I selfishly cried out
Lord Jesus, please heal me.

Thank you, that You took my sin
And died there in my stead
It says you even know my name
Count each hair on my head
So it's reasonable
It just makes sense
You know all about my pain
I'm sure now if I ask
You will make me well again.

POTTERS CLAY

Could it be, I'm beginning to get myself right
From something that happened in our house last night
There was a piece of plasticine stuck on the table
It had been there for days but it wasn't able
'Come on now Jack, move it!' I started to say
It can't move itself, its just made of clay
That word brought a message straight into my ear
Of course, I'm so stupid, the message is clear.

I thought I was clever
That's putting it mild

I find I've not even the brains of a child
What was the message, what did she say?
He is the potter and I am the clay
God is the potter, that's what she said
The potter is living, the clay is just dead
At last I understand, I clearly see
If God is the potter, the clay must be me!
I can't think for tomorrow
There was no yesterday
I just let God mould me
It's better that way.

I make no decisions, all is glorious peace
Like floating on cloudy, cotton wool fleece
I eagerly wait, the clay has no story
I wait to be moulded
Then to God be the glory
Of course being me, I'm just dying to see
If God's going to mould me, what will I be?
I could burst out laughing, a true revelation
I have to die to be God's creation.

MY FRIEND

Dear Lord
Victorious, happy and glorious
I want to sing my praises to You
Wonderful, wonderful
To know you is wonderful
I want to sing my praises to You

Beautiful counsellor
Gracious deliverer
My loving words, never end
All these words describe You
They tell how I love You
But I think of You most
As my friend.

ON THAT DAY

The day is coming nearer
When I'll be with the Lord
The day is soon upon us
He is pouring out His word
He is pouring out His spirit
His light shines from above
The living light of Jesus
Full of love, love, love.

There's a great reunion pending
When I'll be with my Lord
Days one by one are ending
Glory to my Lord
I am praying for you, dear friend
Have you seen the light?
Are you ready, dear friend,
If you have to go tonight?

The day is coming nearer
Let us march up to our Lord

Let's give thanks for His salvation
When He cleansed us with His blood
Let our faces be reflections
Of that great light from above
The living light of Jesus
Full of love, love, love.

CONVERSATION

Here I am Lord, here I am
What are you saying to me?
I try to push You aside but You won't let go
What are You saying to me?

You demand my attention
I can't understand which are Your thoughts
Which are mine
What are You saying to me?

The day You first called me
I wanted to go
No matter where it would be
Now I am waiting, longing to know
What are You saying to me?

In my new life
There's a deep love, a yearning
A longing to do Thy will
Now I am burning, I'm waiting, I'm still
Lord, what are You say to me?

TASK FORCE

How many times since history began
Have we read of the great task force of man?
Young men in their prime, sent off to war
The best years of their lives, spent on some foreign
shore
From the hardest trained soldiers
Their strong muscles twitching
To the newest recruits, serving food in the kitchen
Each one has his use, has his part to play
Each one must be ready, this might be the day
Each weak but training hour by hour
United, spell courage, endurance and power
It's thrilling, exciting, these young men are keen
They're moulded together as a fighting machine.

I've read about forces much stronger than man
Forces in power since this world began
Forces that were earth's very creation
Forces whose power would move a whole nation
Have you read how God's men marched round a town
With a blow of their trumpets, the walls all fell down
Have you read how a young boy, standing alone
Changed the fate of a nation with one little stone
Ah! But that was then, I hear voices sneer
God moved His people but it can't happen here
As I read and understand stories of old
There's a much greater story yet to be told
If you believe in one story, you must read it all
Without flexing a muscle make your enemies fall
It's thrilling, exciting, these stories are true

The force of that power can be flowing through you.

The men in the Bible we no saintly crowd
They weren't seen wearing a halo or praying out loud
They were just normal, full of mistakes
Cheating, lying, looking for breaks
They weren't angels from heaven
They wore no diadem
But the power of God was working through them.
Even the leaders weren't all they should be
Just normal faults I'm sure you'll agree
But because they were God's people, acknowledged
God's power
God was with them and saved them in their needy hour
They just trusted the Lord, Knew what he could do
That same conquering power can be flowing through
you.
All through time, since creation began
Good and evil have battled each other, through man
When God's people were so bad, Satan thought he had
won
Then God saved us all by sending His Son
Jesus died for our sin, by shedding His blood
Evil was beaten by the power of good
By believing in Jesus, you know what that's done
You're heirs of the Father, co-heirs with the Son
As children of God, we can change Satan's course
Let God's power be flowing through this great task
force
Though outnumbered, victory will be our reward
As united we go, in the name of the Lord.

THE PROPOSAL

How I wish, how I long, to give new life
Let's start from today, say you'll be my wife
All those yesterdays might not have been
No one will remember, your slate is wiped clean
Please, from now, start all over, start living anew
You trusting in Me, Me trusting in you,

Up to today you have known many sorrows
Learn from the lessons
Let's share all our tomorrows
I don't really care about what people say
What's lived, now is gone
I love you today.
There's no comfort for you living alone
Let he who has no sin
Cast the first stone
Maybe you'll tell me, as time passes by
But don't feel you have to
Then you don't have to lie.

Please, my love, please let's start a new life
I want to protect you from trouble and strife
Is there something much deeper
Perhaps from the start
Something in your past
That just broke your heart.

I know you're just human, so I won't pretend
Your love may waiver
Your love may just bend

But My love is strong, make no mistake
Love may bend or waiver
But My love won't break.

Just 'tell Me' when you feel how my love is in pain
Just promise you won't let it happen again
Throw out all the rubbish
With your yesterdays in it
Start a new life from now
From this very minute.

DYING TO LIVE FOR JESUS

Tinker, tailor, soldier, sailor
Black, brown, coloured and white
Members of this congregation
All one in Christ tonight
We answered the call
We saw the need
As to us, God's love unfurled
Our hearts replied as the eyes of God
Searched throughout the world
Send me, send me
Here I am, send me
Send me, send me
I will give you my all, send me.

Like Matthew, Mark, Luke and John
Like Peter, James and Paul
From vastly different walks of life
God's love unites us all

God loved the world
He sent His Son
He died and now we're free
Who will go, tell the good news
For His love we cry, send me
Send me, send me
Though my all is small, send me.

We are happy to be in the family of God
With love our lives lay down
On that day of days
We will kneel at His feet
Bow our heads to receive the crown
We will praise the Lord
The King of Kings
Giving thanks for a job well done
As the love of God
Manifest in His Son
By His Spirit cried
God send me
Send me, send me
I'm the one, here I am, send me
Send me, send me
I will go, I am the Lamb, send me.

As time runs out
In these last days
God's army needs you too
Whoever you are, whatever your name
Jesus died for you
All glory and honour and power to God
In Jesus name we fight

You answer the call
Get your armour on
And sing with all you're might
Send me, send me
Here I am, I will go, send me
Here I am precious Lord
Send me.

BORN AGAIN

When I first met Jesus
He was just a feeling, growing deep inside
Like the Virgin Mary
I had done nothing
But his love I couldn't hide
Like a mother heavy ladened
I knew this life would bring me tears of pain
But as this life developed
There would be joy and I was born again.

Like a baby in a manger
My life in Christ was very weak at first
I did a lot of crying
Needing lots of food
And milk to quench my thirst
As I grew with Jesus
There were more smiles
He taught me words to say
From His word He taught me to say 'Daddy'
From His example, I learned how to pray.

When any danger threatened
He would lift me up
And take good care of me
And when I was lonely
He would come and keep me company
Like any baby growing
There'd be times when I would fall
Or do things wrong
But because my Father loves me
He would take my hand and say
'Now come along'.

When I was naughty
He would let me wander
I would be in trouble soon enough
Then I would run back to my Daddy
And find that His stern face
Was just a bluff
He would take me in His arms
And kiss me better
I would feel at peace deep down inside
I'll keep my hand in His, we'll walk together
I'll glow with love, contentment, joy and pride.
Now I'm grown up, I want to work for Jesus
There must be something He wants me to do
And though I'm not really very clever
My Jesus will be there to help me through
Because He's there
My work will seem so easy
As I give my life
I won't suffer loss
Through everything

I know my Jesus loves me
Because He died for me
Upon the cross.

LOVE

Where did all this love come from?
I never had it before
It began with a trickle
Now it's a rush
Like winters ice, during spring thaw
It began with a smile
Then I added a song
Now I'm wanting to dance all the time
I feel like I just want to hug everybody
And my words all come out in rhyme.

I know what happened
I got to know Jesus
I learned how He saved me from sin
So I got baptised
The water was lovely
Now I want everyone to jump in
I only have time to think thoughts about Jesus
Look what's happened since I heard His name
The old me has died, I'm here resurrected
With love, burning up like a flame.
Jesus now is my permanent lodger
He's paid full price for His board
The old me was kicked out
I say 'good riddance'

There's only rooms for my Lord!
He's taken me over
I have no say
He has cleansed all my rooms from sin
Overnight I found, I'd stopped drinking and smoking
I don't want any dirt to get in.

Let me tell you the secret
The whole world can know
The old me is waiting and still
The new me is waiting, listening for Jesus
Ready to move at His will
Do you know what to do, to get some of this love?
It's for all, not just me, that He came
Lift up both arms
Call out, 'Jesus I need you'
And for evermore just praise His name.

<u>GOD IS</u>

God is ever faithful
God is ever true
God is waiting patiently
To hear a word from you
He is waiting to deliver
He waits to hear you say
He promises to answer
All you have to do is pray.

God is always truthful
God is always kind

God will undertake to help
Whatever's on your mind
His gentleness is life itself
His love is always there
He will never let you down
When you go to Him in prayer.

God is all forgiving
God is full of power
God is comfort in your need
However late the hour
Share your laughter
Share your tears
Share your hopes and your fears
You'll soon find out that God is there
He will keep you in His care
When you go to Him in prayer
God is God, God is.

Hebrews 11 vs 6

THE ARK OF GOD

The end of the world is nigh
An all too familiar cry
As Noah cried, the neighbours laughed
They said 'Come and watch this'
'Old Noah's gone daft'
Where is there water
To float that big craft?
He says 'The end of the world is nigh'

Noah believed what God has said
Soon everyone in the world would be dead
He knew, God had told him
To build a big boat
Though there was no water
To make the thing float
He believed, as he heard all his neighbours gloat
The end of the world is nigh.

Noah worked on, day by day
He was building, preparing the way
He instructed his family, what they should do
They collected the animals, two by two
Together they looked a peculiar crew
But the end of the world was nigh.

In God's word, the Bible, were told
Those revealing stories of old
We can see the predictions all coming true
The Bible tells us what we must do
I've got my boat, what about you?
The end of the world is nigh.

Now don't panic, but don't start to chaff
Think of Noah. Who had the last laugh?
Because God loved the world
His Son Jesus died
Now the big boat called 'Faith'
Floats along on life's tide
There's plenty of room for God's people inside
The end of the world is nigh.

In faith Noah made a new start
By faith of God's word in his heart
Faith is the answer, faith is the key
Faith, that Jesus, God's Son died
Because He loves me
In God's boat of faith, I'm so grateful to be
The end of the world is nigh.

When in faith, you can't see that it's there
But, when in faith, you cast off all your care
Don't look down at the sea of the world's fear and
doubt
When a wave washes over
Look up, pray out
When we're all on board
There will be a glad shout
The end of the world is nigh.

WALKING IN LOVE

Why are you weary my love, my friend?
What has caused you to frown?
With love I watch from a distance
I see when your hands hang down
You've drawn yourself away, alone
Something hurting, your eyes have shown
Something, maybe even to you, unknown
Jesus told me to love you.

At times when you're weary my love, my friend
There's always someone there

There's always someone who sees you down
And lifts you up on a prayer
God hears the sound of the deepest sigh
He knows the need and the angels fly
It's not for us to question why
Jesus told me to love you.

If ever you're weary my love, my friend
Remember this special love
Not the love of the world as the world knows love
But direct from heaven above
This kind of love does not offend
Love that wants to heal and mend
Love that lays down His life for a friend
Jesus told me to love you.

When you are weary my love, my friend
Rest in the love that is there
Try to remember 'my burden is light
My cross not too heavy to bear'
Draw yourself away, be still
Quiet your mind and wait until
With the water life, your cup He'll fill
Jesus told me He loves you.

STILL LEARNING

I've learned to praise God
To yield to His will
I thought I had, at least until
Things seemed to go wrong
My grumbling and moaning didn't take long.

When days start with sunshine
All bright and breezy
To praise God for all things
To love Him is easy
But what about days
When the sun turns to rain
On bitter, cold days
Do I praise God again?

Do I praise God
For sending rain to grow food?
Even bitter cold days
Are sent for our good
Even when things don't seem to go right
Even when I'm worried
And can't sleep all night
Even for troubles close to my heart
Even as my world seems to be falling apart
Can I believe God is loving me still?
Can I still say I yield to God's will?

Then I see Jesus, hung on that tree
I see His body broken for me
I see His tormentors, I feel His pain

The blood, where they stabbed Him again and again
I see His body, battered and shaken
I hear Him cry out, "Am I forsaken?"

Even this horror is part of God's plan
For our sin, there had to die, one perfect man
He'd healed so many people
He is God's Son
Yet He yielded and cried to God
"Thy will be done."

So He yielded and finally shuddered and died
Then God raised Him up to stand by His side
Even death has no power over God's will
Jesus was dead, now is living still
So let me not question God or His ways
I yield
And in all things my God I will praise.

FOR THE PRAYER BOOK

We come to You Lord
With praise and with prayer
We worship You Lord
We know that You care
We bring these requests
For hope and salvation
For each person mentioned
Each quarrelling nation
We know You can do it Lord
You can comfort them all

There's not one request
That's too big or small.

The miracles done by You
All those years ago
Are still done in our time
In ourselves, so we know
There's no love so unchanging
No promise so true
As these gifts from our Father
As He gave them through You
We now give You our problems
Our suffering, our pain
We know by Your promise
You'll restore us again.

We thank You now Lord
We thank Jesus the Son
Whatever we need Lord
Thy will be done.

THOUGHTS IN THE NIGHT

Dear Lord, I awake crying to You
Dear Lord, please tell me what I can do
Here I am Lord, I'm waiting, longing to know
What can I do Lord, where can I go?
Here I am Lord, still waiting, asleep in my bed
My throat now is aching, with words to be said
Can I say I love You, in my own special way

I want You to know Lord, how I'm feeling today
I'm kneeling, I'm praying, I'm giving my all
I hear You dear Father, I answer Your call
Dear Lord, my Master, my Saviour, my Friend
I love You sweet Jesus
This love has no end.

THANKS

Dear Lord, sweet Jesus
As I kneel to pray
I just want to say thanks for this glorious day
I had a feeling
With the first rays of light
It would be one of those days
Things would just turn out right
And they did
Thanks to You Lord
It's so clearly true
All things go right Lord
When I'm trusting in You
How great is my life, since I've learned
Just to say
I'm trusting in You Lord
Then leave it that way
Dear Lord, my sweet Jesus
It's lovely to pray
I love You and thanks
It's a beautiful day.

SACRIFICE IN PRACTICE

Soldiers marching to the front
Stamping a rhythm together
The dreary routine they've practised so long
In all kinds of inclement weather
They've practiced so much
They jump and run
As the sergeants whistles peep
They've practised so much
I've heard them say
They can do it in their sleep
But now this is the real thing
Their bullets and guns are real
Do you think it could be, they've practised so long
They've forgotten how to feel?

As they crouch in their trench, in the dark of the night
Feeling enemy all around
What do they think as they lie in wait
Their bodies pressed close to the ground?
Some will think of the wife and kids
Others will think of Mum
Others will think of their 'last night out'
Or the power of holding a gun
No doubt all will know a moment of fear
As they wait for the battle to start
How many will suddenly cry out to God?
With a silent cry, deep in their heart
It won't be because they are cowards
That they cry as help to seek
It won't be because they don't know what to do

Or because their bodies are weak
It will be because, as they lay side by side
The long and the short and the tall
The dark makes the enemy seem so big
And suddenly they feel small.

So they cry out to God to strengthen their hearts
To give them the power to fight
As the whistles peep, they jump and run
Running blindly as soldiers might
They run forward because they are trained that way
They've practised time after time
The adrenaline high, driving them on
But keeping their comrades in line
They fight hard and long
With no sense of pain
Determined they're going to win
They trained so well, they follow the leader
Not thinking once to give in
As each one overcomes, the power of darkness
As his eyes get used to the night
As the black turns to grey, then the grey becomes
lighter
Then the dawn brings the sun's burst of light.

God, grant each soldier strength to remember his
training
Let his cry to God not go amiss
If he dies in the battle, he will go up to 'glory'
For greater love hath no man than this.

Lightning Source UK Ltd.
Milton Keynes UK
UKHW020622020223
416354UK00010B/1465

9 798787 266658